YOUR HOUSE KEYS ARE IN THE DRYER

A PARENTING HAIKU BOOK

Alisha Gaddis

Post Hill
PRESS

A POST HILL PRESS BOOK
ISBN: 978-1-63758-611-2
ISBN (eBook): 978-1-63758-612-9

Your House Keys are in the Dryer:
A Parenting Haiku Book
© 2022 by Alisha Gaddis
All Rights Reserved

Cover design by Tiffani Shea

Post Hill Press
New York • Nashville
posthillpress.com

Published in the United States of America

1 2 3 4 5 6 7 8 9 10

Dedicated to the
Pile and pandemic parenting.

PREFACE

Written by moms, *Your House Keys are in the Dryer: A Parenting Haiku Book* describes the biggest job in the world…in the fewest syllables possible.

Distilling motherhood into the traditional 5-7-5 haiku format was thrilling, exhausting, and all these busy mamas had time for.

> *Writing one haiku*
> *In between lunch, dance, nap, school*
> *Where'd I put those keys*

Laugh, cry, and relate with these flashes of the fleeting moments we call parenthood.

what no one tells you

(and there is so much untold):

"mama" is a verb

❀Samantha Speiller

My morning coffee

My co-parent. Reheated

For the 13th time.

🌸 Laurissa James

It's quiet right now.

I sit down to drink coffee.

Fate and my kid laugh.

🌸Martina Papinchak

I pour milk into

The Elsa cup. Oh dear god,

Elsa is for juice.

✿Laurissa James

That thing where you go

To the grocery store just

To have alone time.

🌸Liz Kocan

Every day I fear

I will damage you with words

I love you, sorry.

🌸Lori Elberg

Love, Frustration, Love

Frustration, Love, Frustration

Love, Frustration, Love

🌸 Jessica Glassberg

shavasana? or

did I nap hard at yoga?

I will never tell

✿Kate Tellers

Sitting in traffic

May as well be vacation

For my tired ass

🌸 Joy Rumore

Motherhood is not

too bad, especially if

you like company

🌸Emily Barth Isler

No no no no no

No no no no no no no

No no no please no

🌸Miellyn Fitzwater Barrows

"Do you have to pee?"

"No," she says dancing about

Soon her pants are wet

🌸Dava Krause

Parenting is hard

Blood, pee, crying, and vomit

And that's just from me

🌸Jessica Delfino

if I told you that

this chicken is from Popeye's

would you eat it then?

🌸Kate Tellers

What? Me...? Who am I?

...I seem to have forgotten.

Hmm, I used to know.

🌼 Jessica Glassberg

I love you so much

I just want to pee alone

Just for one moment

●Dori Howard

I observe the wall

next to your bed, many specks

from inside your nose

🌸Tess Lynch

What's that on my face?

Marker? Sauce? Toothpaste? Poop? Glue?

...How long's it been there?

🌸Jessica Glassberg

When I look at you

I see my whole family

You smile history.

✿Lori Elberg

Never wanted kids.

My friend's baby changed my mind.

What if he hadn't?

🌸Amanda Hirsch

"Will you kids please stop

all your screaming!?" she screamed. The

irony was rich.

●Liz Kocan

"Hey mom, look at me!"

Stopping my own momentum

Jump AND spin, bravo.

Ilana Cohn

Through my C-section

Played "House of the Rising Sun"

Oh my, doctor, why?

🌸Rachelle Crum

Mom. Mom? Where are you?

Mom! Hello?! Hey Mommy? MOM!!!!!

Who locked the bathroom?

🌸Laurissa James

You bite my nipple.

It hurts so much, tears fall down.

You then smile with glee.

⚘Jennie Sheffield

Back to school again

At last, I have peace, quiet

I miss you so much

           ❀Jen McCreary

do you want to know

how to be invisible?

just hold a baby

🌸Lisa Brenner

I am the keeper

Of your first years' memories

A gift just for me

🌸Jen McCreary

all that stands between

a good day and a bad day?

the right color cup.

🌸Samantha Speiller

F*ck, am I too late?

I want to participate

But Mom-ing stops me

🌸Carissa Kosta

(Stepmotherhood)

Took me to their spot

They asked me to live with them

Hope I get this right

🌸Samantha Aluise

Pickles, cheese, olives,

seaweed, pretzels, salami;

Snacks for every meal.

🌸Martina Papinchak

"Want to play mermaids?"

"Only if it's in Cancun."

"What is a Cancun?"

✿Steph Garcia

I grew those small hands

That now destroy everything

I birthed Godzilla

🌸Gwen Mesco

When will we get there?

Mama when will we get there?

When will we get there?

🌸 Taylor Miller

Legs swing on a cold

Silver table of unknown,

Cut to cries of hope.

🌸Katya Lidsky

I look at you with

the eyes my mom once watched me.

Now I understand.

❀Laurissa James

A pea. A nugget

Touch by accident. My child

Is now scarred for life.

◆Laurissa James

I have hopes and dreams

For my precious kids, of course.

My own dreams faded.

🌸Jessica Glassberg

Mom, I forgive you

Because now I understand

Parenthood is hard.

✿Lori Elberg

Okay okay o-

Oh, that's what you meant? Oh, uh

Yeah no no way no

🏵Miellyn Fitzwater Barrows

Mommy help! She cries

I fear she is in danger

No. She just wants snacks.

🌸 Dava Krause

No you can't have snacks

Pretty please just eat dinner

that bite did not count.

🏵 Dori Howard

Hey, put that down please

Shoes do not go in our mouths

Could you maybe nap?

🌸Miellyn Fitzwater Barrows

Hell is when your kid

Tells you the rules to a game

they just made up now

🌸Emily Barth Isler

Soap! Soap! I said soap!

You need soap to wash your hands!

Don't just wet the germs!

🌸 Joy Rumore

Cool mom at the park

in dry-clean only outfit

I'll just stay quiet

●Tess Lynch

Medical visit

Essentially a spa day

I even dozed off

🌸 Joy Rumore

Go to sleep now please

Naps are for big kids—like us!

Yes! I will show you.

✿Alisha Gaddis

Pre-kids, never lied

now I do it easily:

shoot! iPad's broken!

❀Kate Tellers

thank god we are here

on this R train where no one

thinks it's your diaper

🌸Kate Tellers

Does she look like me?

I hope she's smarter than me.

Smarter than I? Please.

🌸 Jessica Glassberg

We brush teeth daily

There's No Negotiation

You want teeth like Dad?

🌸 Lori Elberg

The calendar ends

"Do we all die," she asked me?

The laughs keep coming.

Ilana Cohn

She said "Click subscribe"

To one of her Zoom teachers

"And give a thumbs up"

☙Rachelle Crum

That puddle is new.

A melted ice cube? I wish.

Potty training fail.

🌸Laurissa James

Mommy! Wipe my butt!

You need to learn soon yourself.

Eww. Gross. You Do It!

🌸Jennie Sheffield

Elsa, Anna, Belle

Tiana, Snow White. How did

I lose this battle?

🌸Dori Howard

You outgrow your clothes

So quickly that I miss them

But not the diapers

🌸 Jen McCreary

Why all the screaming?

I shut the door, brief silence.

Banging and screaming

🌸Jennie Sheffield

Why does it take you

Hours to poop but seconds

To destroy your room?

❀ Jen McCreary

Can I have a hug?

No, you're not too big for that.

Off please! Leg's asleep!

✿Alisha Gaddis

snap crackle and pop

take care of your pelvic floor

i'm fun at parties

🌸Lisa Brenner

light up shoes are fun

they make her smile 'til they don't

goodbye fifty bucks

❀Samantha Speiller

Mama. Mommy! MOM.

MAAAA-AAAA-AAAA-
AAAA-AAAA-AAAA-MA!

I need some water

🌼Gwen Mesco

Screen time is for fools

They told me once in a class

And fool, I now am

🌸 Steph Garcia

Stop, you will break that!

There, it broke, are you happy?

Will you stop crying?

🌼Martina Papinchak

Yep. Okay. Yes. No.

Can't hear you, what did you say?

Go ask your father.

🌸 Alisha Gaddis

Please. Stop whining, please.

Okay, I wouldn't say please.

And I'd be screaming.

🌸Jessica Glassberg

I would pay thousands

To never again have to

Hear the hot dog song

🌸 Jen McCreary

"why do i exist?"

"because i invented you."

"can i watch tv?"

🌸Lisa Brenner

Come over here please.

Look at me when I'm talking.

No, you can't eat rocks.

●Alisha Gaddis

Someone watching me

As I pee or as I work.

Always constant eyes.

✿Jennie Sheffield

went to a movie

came back to 91 texts

Vi's son lost a tooth!

🌸Kate Tellers

No no no no no

No no no no no no no

No no no no nope

◆Miellyn Fitzwater Barrows

one thing I wish is

that you understood money

I'd pay you to nap

🌸Kate Tellers

Underwear clad lad

Blow up dino on his back

Runs amok in yard

✿ Joy Rumore

what is a golem

i think that i might be one

i used to be cute

🌼Lisa Brenner

TV time is done.

I am not a bad mother.

Yes, I am a queen.

✿Jennie Sheffield

Stop pulling my hair...

Now, let go of my boobies.

Please give Mom her space.

❀Lori Elberg

Why did they change math?

Old math was perfectly fine,

what the shit is this?

❀Liz Kocan

My son is now nine

He has tried to call me "bro"

Cut it out please, dude

🌸Rachelle Crum

Hair toss. Eye roll. <huff>

Expert Exasperation.

You can't be just six.

🌸Laurissa James

Pieces of glitter

In my hair and on the chair.

Glitter everywhere.

✿ Jennie Sheffield

poo in my pocket

my secret, my shame, her turd

(how did it get there?)

✿Samantha Speiller

First night home jitters

We slept in our rocking chair

Couldn't put her down

🌸Samantha Aluise

First date in a year.

The babysitter canceled.

Can I go alone?

🌸Martina Papinchak

When lying in bed

Ouch! Crayons, crumbs, Legos, pee?

Goodbye, sexy time.

Alisha Gaddis

You light up my world

You light up all your artwork

Oh God! House on fire!

Steph Garcia

INT. BEDROOM — MIDNIGHT

MONSTER enters from closet.

MOM zaps it. BLACKOUT.

🌸 Gwen Mesco

Oh babe, that was sweet

Thank you for saying thank you

You are the best kid

⬤ Miellyn Fitzwater Barrows

thanks for the run down

of Paw Patrol I needed

that information

☘Kate Tellers

Stop! Watch out for cars.

Hold my hand to cross the road.

Safety's exhausting.

🌸Alisha Gaddis

Why? Why? Why? Why? Why?

Why do you keep asking me?

Beats me. I don't know!

●Miellyn Fitzwater Barrows

You're the best of us.

Dad thinks you are photoshopped.

Did we create you?

 ❀ Lori Elberg

It floats to the top.

Poop hanging with the bath toys.

Oh please, not again.

◈Jennie Sheffield

"where is the ipad?"

"finish your chicken first please."

"i'm asking daddy."

🌸 Lisa Brenner

My spawn, who are you?

Growing into a human

Will you still love me?

🏵 Carissa Kosta

This baby is big

Sonograms reporting LARGE

Born just the right size

🌸 Samantha Aluise

You left a present

In my boot, found while you slept

One perfect blue block

🌸Gwen Mesco

paid ninety dollars

so that a teenager could

Netflix on our couch

🌸Kate Tellers

Sex with your partner.

Rarely ever in the mood.

Fake it to make it!

●Martina Papinchak

Yes yes yes yes yes

Yes okay sure okay yes

Yes yes yep yes YES

✿Miellyn Fitzwater Barrows

for the love of all

that is good and holy please

try one goddamn bite

🌸Kate Tellers

it's a damn shitshow

sleep-when-they-sleep is a lie

but blink and they're five

🌸Lisa Brenner

Goodnight, I love you.

Water, story, stuffy, check!

One more hug? Always.

⚘Alisha Gaddis

the irony of

"good morning" sung sweetly at

4:30 AM

🌸 Samantha Speiller

I once slept alone

Now it's with octopuses

Wait... Those are my kids

🌸Steph Garcia

Three AM, rocking

Your hand curls around my thumb

Us against the night

🌸Gwen Mesco

I put you to sleep

Open a bottle of wine

And wake you up. Sigh.

🌸Steph Garcia

Your smile is perfect

Even when it's 3 AM

And you want a snack

🌸Jen McCreary

Restless nights rocking

Baby back to sleep, you're up

Now scrolling, in deep

🌸Ilana Cohn

My sweet baby girl

I love your strength, power, voice

But it's 4 AM.

🌸Laurissa James

she wakes when it's dark

Demanding milk and my soul

I am so tired

🌸 Dava Krause

Waiting for bedtime,

but then after you go down,

I scroll pics of you.

🌸 Julia Price Baron

when you are in bed

I try to do everything

but mostly TikTok

❀Kate Tellers

I sleep in my bra.

I squirt milk in my babe's eye.

Sometimes on purpose.

✿Jessica Glassberg

Why are you so cute

When you are asleep my dear

Because you're quiet?

✿Emily Barth Isler

no one told me that

it would be such hard work to

make you unconscious

❀Kate Tellers

We giggle and gaze.

You drift to sleep in my arms.

My heart swells with love.

✿Jennie Sheffield

You hug your stuffies

Some day you will outgrow them

Why am I crying?

● Jen McCreary

I love my children.

Yes, even when they hate me.

I'm Mommy. Always.

☘Jessica Glassberg

I love you, too, kid

More than you can understand

One day you will know

🌸Miellyn Fitzwater Barrows

ABOUT THE AUTHOR

Author photo by:
Jesse Ashton

Alisha Gaddis is a red-haired, feisty empath. She has won multiple Grammy and Emmy awards and published numerous books on a plethora of topics ranging from weaning and acting to stepparenting and periods. She has acted in and written for many television shows, movies, and live productions. She delights in her extreme multi-hyphenate "job title." She and her little family split their time between Los Angeles, Columbus, IN, and Paris.

This haiku book was absolutely inspired by her lack of time and still wanting to do it all with her mom friends.

CONTRIBUTOR BIOS

Samantha Aluise is a Mom of all trades and Spiritual Counselor who can be found body surfing waves on the beach with her husband and two rascally young daughters. In Samantha's work through Enlighten Mentoring, she empowers and guides her clients on their journey in life. She believes everyone should feel loved and worthy and safe.

Julia Price Baron is a writer, creative director, and filmmaker who lives with her husband, six-year-old daughter, and eleven-year-old cat in Brooklyn, NY.

Miellyn Barrows has written about video games for VICE, celebrities for VH1.com, true crime for Investigation Discovery, public health for The Milken Institute, historical artifacts for Smithsonian, and science for National Geographic. She also invented the mom joke. (They're like dad jokes, but they don't stink.)

Emily Barth Isler is the author of *AfterMath*, a middle-grade novel Amy Schumer calls "a gift to the culture." She also writes about sustainable and ethically sourced beauty for magazines and websites, lives in Los Angeles with her family, and can be found at emilybarthisler.com

Lisa Brenner is a Los Angeles-based writer and a Senior Creative Producer at Spotify. She makes kids' podcasts, writes essays and songs, and if you think you heard her on NPR giving a potato latke tutorial, you definitely did.

Ilana Cohn is a Los Angeles-based director, writer, and actor who created *Overdue* for AwesomenessTV. She has been seen on *It's Always Sunny in Philadelphia* and has done voices on Comedy Central's *South Park*.

Rachelle Crum is a writer and mom of two in Los Angeles. She grew up in Pennsylvania, graduated from the University of Delaware, and still has a Stone Balloon mug.

@JessicaDelfino is a mom, marketing director, host of the weekly Mom Report on Pocono 96.7 FM, and a freelance writer for *The New York Times* and more by day. At night, she's a delightfully twisted comedic musician who sings original "dirty folk rock" songs and mutilated classic rock covers.

Lori Elberg is an award-winning writer-director raised in the shopping malls of Northern New Jersey, which explains her sense of humor and wardrobe choices. She has created animated series, written for film and television, and her husband has claimed that she made their daughter on Photoshop because she combines all their best qualities.

Steph Garcia is a comedy writer who has written for a talk show, a kid's show, and a sketch show. She's also a mom of two who loves to do puzzles with thousands of pieces.

Jessica Glassberg is an award-winning writer, producer, director, and stand-up comedian. Her credits include writing for NBC, Lifetime, Disney, UPtv, Amy Poehler, Nick Offerman, and Jerry Lewis, and, in addition to an array of televised and digital content, she has also produced two children.

Amanda Hirsch is on a mission to fill the world with women's stories, which she does as the CEO and founder of women's storytelling company Mighty Forces, a story coach to women leaders, and as a writer. You can learn more about her work at amandahirsch.com.

Dori Howard is an entrepreneur, executive, and activist originally from New Jersey who now calls Los Angeles home. She fights every day to make the world a better place for her two young girls, Mila and Ruby (who she also fights with every day).

Laurissa James is a Los Angeles-based writer and television producer who delights in creating silly songs, stories, and fake Netflix shows with her young daughter. Her side passions include cooking, wellness coaching, and trying to convince her east coast friends to move to LA.

Liz Kocan is a writer based in Western Massachusetts. She spends her life picking up after everyone.

Carissa Kosta is a Wisconsin-grown Greek-immigrant spawn who recently wrapped ABC's *United We Fall* starring Jane Curtin. Before that, she co-created a series called *Flip A Bitch*, which reached hundreds of thousands of people when it was featured on *Cosmopolitan* online. She also had two babies ripped out of her stomach.

With a background in stand-up comedy, Dava Krause is the creator, writer, and producer of *Baby Steps*, a comedy about motherhood and feminism which won "Best Pilot" at Dances with Films 2021. She currently works in advertising as a post producer, and you can find her complaining about her children on Instagram.com/davakrause

Katya Lidsky writes books, essays, TV shows, and lists (she loves lists). She is the host of *The Animal That Changed You* podcast, runs a writer-centric production company called Pesky Moon, and is very much a dog person. Follow her @KatyaLidsky

Tess Lynch is a writer (*Grantland, GOOD, n+1, New York Magazine*) and podcaster (ESPN's *Girls in Hoodies*, iHeart Radio's *Night Call*). She is a four-time drunk narrator on Comedy Central's *Drunk History*, yet amazingly lives on with a fully functional liver—as well as her husband and children—in Los Angeles.

Jen McCreary is a writer and editor living in Southern California with her family, their dog, and a yard full of fruit trees.

Gwen Mesco is a writer and mother based in Los Angeles. For more of her short-form work, visit her Twitter at @messily.

Taylor O Miller is an award-winning documentary photographer and filmmaker. She is the co-founder of Slamdance Unstoppable, a program created by and for filmmakers with visible and non-visible disabilities.

Martina Lynne Papinchak published her first poem in the *Idaho Statesman* when she was six years old and is thrilled to be reviving her poetry career now that she lives in Los Angeles with her husband and their daughter. A graduate of Yale University, Martina writes and develops projects for novels, film, and television and is currently creating a pilot for ABC.

Joy Rumore is a mom/wife/tattooer/illustrator/podcaster/editor/writer living in Long Beach, California, with her family. She drinks a lot of coffee and talks to squirrels.

With a background in sketch comedy and a BFA from NYU, Jennie Sheffield is a creator, writer, and producer with her latest creation *Silverlake In Utero*, also about motherhood, which can be found on YouTube. She resides in LA and juggles writing gigs, auditions, owning a Pilates business, and being a mother of two humans, a cat, and a dog.

Sam Spieller is an improviser (formally of Upright Citizens Brigade in NYC), writer (*ScaryMommy* and *Reductress*), and mother to a delightfully rebellious five-year-old girl. She is embarrassingly proud of her ever-growing following on Tik Tok, where she is a self-pro-claimed macro-influencer.

Kate Tellers is a writer, storyteller, host, and co-author of *How to Tell a Story: The Essential Guide to Memorable Storytelling from The Moth* (Crown). Her writing has appeared in *McSweeney's* and the *New Yorker*. Obviously, she's also a mom. @thekatetellers

Dawn White is a mother, an entertainment executive, artist manager, tv/film producer, and freelance writer. She enjoys cooking, yoga, and although she loves her son with all her heart and soul, let's be real: some days are hard as a mofo.

SPECIAL THANKS

Special Thanks: THE PILE!!! All the amazing mamas who wrote for the book—I have never received paperwork back faster from any group of people, ever! You moms can do anything (but it's ok to be tired and take a rest from doing it all)! Sara Camilli, Raquel D'Apice for coming up with the epic book title; Miellyn, Debby Englander, and the team; my husband; and most importantly—my sweet, Indiana Maven, who exhausts and propels me. She is the magic I made that makes me want to keep making.